MESSAGES

An Invitation for Humanity to Evolve

GARY LEE CHRISTENSEN

An Imprint for GracePoint Publishing, a
Division of GracePoint Matrix, LLC
624 S. Cascade Ave. #201
Colorado Springs, CO
80920

EMP⊙WER
P R E S S

Email: Admin@GracePointMatrix.
com SAN # 991-6032
ISBN: 978-1-951694-06-7
eISBN: 978-1-951694-07-4
Books may be purchased for educational,
business, or sales promotional use.
For bulk order requests and price schedule
contact: Orders@GracePointPublishing.com
Printed in the United States of America.

INTRODUCTION

These messages were received by Gary Lee Christensen, who was born in 1959 on the Pine Ridge Reservation in South Dakota. He lived during the time of the relocation period of the tribes during the 1950s, and upon returning to the peoples (Lakotas), he found his ancestral path called the Red Road, *C'unku Luta* (Chun-koo Loo-tah)[1]. Walking the path of the Red Road is a way of acting respectful to life that directs us in community. Through his spiritual seeking he encountered beings he refers to as The Star People and was given visions and messages to convey to the world. *I want this!*

This is a story of a man's search for understanding spirituality through contact

---

1   Once introduced, English and Lakota terms will be used interchangeably throughout the book. See Glossary: Pronunciation and Translation for Lakota Words.

and visions received from the *Wic'ahpi Oyate* (Wee-chalk-pee Oi-yah-tay), which means Star Nation in Lakota. From his earliest memories, the *Wic'ahpi Oyate* have always been here, and this book is an account of received wisdom. It has been edited with the intention of keeping the voice of the Star Nation as true to their original transmissions while maintaining industry-standard integrity. All editing in this work has been done to enhance the clarity of the message and not to change the meaning of this important body of information.

BEGINNINGS

Hello, my name is Gary, and I am here to share a message I've been given from forces outside myself. The message was given to me from the ones who have come to be known to me as the Wic'ahpi Oyate, which some call Star People, Alien Nation, or extraterrestrials.

A brief acknowledgment: I am Oglala Lakota. The language used throughout is Lakota and English.

As I wrote this out, I tried to separate the difference between spiritual, paranormal, and universal experiences, but I have concluded there is no separation, as they are all one and the same. Life is a spiritual endeavor, and those seeking spirituality are more inclined to encounter Higher Forces or Beings. These teachings will include not only alien messages given to all people, but also visions and dreams (astral messages) and communications from alien entities that have been given specifically to me. In trying to keep this information within a time frame, I had to break it down into different chapters and references.

So here we are, and this is where my story begins.

CHAPTER ONE

Roots

My parents were both were enrolled members of the federally recognized Lakota tribe. My mother's maiden name was Mabel Man Walks Underground and my father was Phillip Edward Christensen. This is my Native American heritage, and it also explains my connection to nature, alternate universes, dimensions, and realms.

I was given visions at an early age.

My connection to Mother Earth and all her realms gifted me with these visions, messages, and knowledge of astral projection.

Spirit entities that exist throughout the universal realms showed me that my heritage was one of the reasons that I was chosen to share this message from the Wic'ahpi Oyate.

My Native American connection to the Universe is given, as it is to all the great healers of tribal affiliation (Medicine and Holy Men) that are in contact with these same spiritual entities of different dimensions. However, alien entities exist within these same dimension and realms, which means we are not alone. Alien Nations have always been here watching and keeping track of our evolution and advancement as a species, awaiting our eventual maturation to the point that we might take our place within a greater intergalactic community.

I am here to relay messages from an alien entity and share the story as to how these messages have come to be received.

My early childhood between birth and six years old was an important time. These were the first encounters not only with alien entities, but also my first connection to the other spiritual beings within the natural worlds. The earthly realms, as well as the intergalactic, are all one in the same.

One of the beings I encountered was an entity which appeared as a shadow figure with glowing red eyes. Though unknown at this time, the being would play a significant role in my life from this point forward.

My mother and I were very ill during this time, having contracted tuberculosis, and we were placed in the local sanitarium. This led to many changes within my family life as my father and mother separated and divorced. I recovered but my mother had to have her lung scraped and recovery was not forth going for some time after.

At this point I was placed in the care of family members and would not be able to see my mother for many years to come. This would eventually lead to my leaving

South Dakota and the eventual relocation to Washington State. These occurrences and subsequent leaving the ranch where I was cared for, were quite crucial, because it was during this time that the first message was given to me by the Owl People through my connection to the spiritual realm.

Our Lakota culture believes that all life and creatures of the earth are our brothers and sisters. At this early date I would receive my first message from these relatives. This occurrence would bring change once more to my young life.

On that day so long ago, I was playing in the field outside the ranch house near the trees in a wind break when an owl came flying up and landed in one of them. He looked at me and spoke, "They're coming for you!"

I, not knowing people don't speak to owls, asked, "Who? Who's coming for me?" He did not answer me and only flew away.

Later that day my father and grandfather came up the drive and told my caretakers they had come for me, and my life was forever changed once again. I would be relocated to another point on the map, but this would be more significant as it would be my first contact with the alien entities.

CHAPTER TWO

Connection

My grandfather and father had come to South Dakota to collect me and take me to the big city of Spokane, Washington.

I was reunited with my two sisters, which was good for me as I then had siblings to connect to and play with again. My vague, earliest memories were of my mother, sisters, and me.

We lived in a large house in the inner city. At this time, we had many relatives that came to visit, including aunts, uncles, cousins, and family friends. It was a happy time as my grandfather, who had raised my father, favored me, and took me along on his excursions around town.

After his passing I was alone, no longer a favored child, and from this point on pretty much became a loner. This was the beginning of the realization of my connection to and belief in the Wic'ahpi Oyate. At that time the depiction of them was always as alien beings. Historically, at this time, there was the Roswell incident in 1947 and Area 51, built in 1955, which shaped my understanding. In Spokane, I began my research on aliens as my belief, and my questioning began—searching for answers as it were.

What occurred during those early days of life in the city was soon to be concluded. My young life, and what subsequently has come to me, would be my connection to the Wic'ahpi Oyate.

As in most families during this time, everybody had a black and white television which led to an advancement into the space-age futuristic society that we exist in today. Later I will bring into light the future and its connection to forbidden knowledge and science fiction. My sisters were busy with their families and their lives and now I was left to myself to watch a show on the television. The movie I remember was the 1951 original version of The Day the Earth Stood Still. The depiction, as I remember it, was of an alien and his robot being stuck on earth. At one point, after returning to their spaceship, the alien gave a message to the lowly Earthlings about the destruction of self and humanity. After fifty odd years the message still holds interest to me. I have always wanted a copy of this movie as it was so important to my early evolution. This movie enlightened my young mind and placed a seed of awareness that would lead to the occurrences of one very important summer day that would permanently change my life.

On that day, sometime in 1964, the family gathered, and the adults were in the house visiting. They loved playing poker and drinking beer. We children were left to play outside, as the weather was nice on that beautiful summer day.

My siblings and young cousins were running around screaming, hollering, and enjoying their young lives. As children were prone to do back then, they played hide and seek and tag in the yard. I took leave of this play and threw myself down on my back in the green grass. Looking up into the sky, I saw something that would change me forever. There were four metallic discs orbiting above us in the blue sky, just hanging there, suspended above the city in broad daylight. I remember looking around and asking myself, "Am I the only one that is seeing this?" Upon realizing that these four metallic discs were actually floating above me, I resigned myself to watching them. Later,

I often wondered as a witness, What if I had brought attention to this phenomenon instead of keeping it to myself? I watched them hover above me until they finally took leave of their orbit and blipped away in a second. They existed in one moment and then suddenly they were gone.

From that day forward I was a believer and knew they were, and are, very real. My connection with the Wic'ahpi Oyate strengthened as my education and knowledge grew. This spiritual journey would lead eventually to my abduction and would someday gift me with knowledge of the Star People.

CHAPTER THREE

Revolution of Evolution

To put some perspective to the date of the
life and times of me and my generation, we
must acknowledge the impact media has had
on us all. When we moved to the prairie,
I remember witnessing the first light bulb
with electricity. When either the electricity
was hooked up or the bill paid, I remember the lights coming on. The world during
the 1960s was turbulent, and events would
show themselves as displays of power from
what I came to understand was the shadow
government

I remember a family member dragging an old antique radio with a round top into the house. This was a major form of entertainment for all of us. I remember everyone sitting around listening to the radio and the story shows. One of my earliest music memories was Johnny Cash singing the "Ring of Fire" Smart phones, personal computers, and social media were some forms of science fiction at this time, as we did not even have a landline yet.

Up until then, I had never seen a television, but that was about to change. One day, someone brought in a black and white TV. That was a game changer as it brought in the outside world to the prairie and a whole different sense of being!

I was now connected, very aware of the life around me, and a witness to the world events and happenings otherwise not attainable from the ranch. My mind was expanding with the introduction of new technologies, and though I did not know how to tell time, I knew when The Roy Rogers Show was coming on! The beginning of my programming and the subliminal messaging of the media had been inserted.

My first memory of social unrest and political assassinations was the killing of President John Fitzgerald Kennedy. I was understanding a new reality as I watched on that small black and white screen of the television. Why was everyone crying and carrying on that day? The meanderings of my four-year-old brain finally grasped that he had been a great man and that it was a very important date.

Through that black and white box, I would come to see the ways of the world and begin to understand some of the two-leggeds (humans) and their use of control here upon the earth. I began to witness many things: the Civil Rights movement, the Vietnam War, Martin Luther King, Jr.

and his dreams, and Malcolm X with his message. There was also Marilyn Monroe's suicide, President Eisenhower and his message of the military industrial complex, and Robert Kennedy's assassination.

Finally, I witnessed the hippie movement, the Timothy Leary experiments, Bigfoot, Elvis, John Lennon, and the Summer of Love. However, the big one for me was the uprising of the Lakota people and the American Indian Movement on the Pine Ridge Reservation at Wounded Knee.

The technological development of the human race had begun, and an evolution was taking place as we strove to further ourselves by putting men on the moon during the Cold War. In my opinion, we had concluded that we were a racial society and hell bent on the destruction of humanity and the planet. At eight years of age, I became a conscientious objector to war and the systematic exploitation of humanity. I was a little bit different than other children my age.

Also, at this early date, I started having spiritual as well as paranormal experiences that would again set a course in the direction I would be walking for the rest of my days. In the early years, when it was recognized that I was ready to study our culture, I was given an avenue to my heritage. I was sent to a native cultural class to be able to grasp the meaning of who I was and what I was! I remember seeing an article written in a magazine that was titled, "Who are these Lakota and why do they have to mutilate themselves to pray?" In that moment I knew there was something to be understood. There was a sprig of sage nearby and I remember thinking to myself, "I hear they use this in ceremony." I lit the sage and can still remember how the spirit of the plant filled my entire being and took me to another place.

These experiences helped to turn my direction into spiritual seeking and finding my Lakota language, which has been a learning process that I am still involved with every day. Through this communication, alien forces continue to share their message with me that translates as, "I want to lay down tracks to what this is truly all about."

I also want to mention that today's technological leaps with media, computers, and iPhones are a direct result of knowledge gained through alien technology. That advancement was given so that we as a species could evolve to a point where we will be recognized as candidates for an intergalactic community and given the gateway to the stars. Questioning and/or believing that we are the only living species of the Universe is quite ludicrous and shameful.

This message entails that alien life or alien beings have been here forever and have been watching over us as we have evolved.

They are waiting for humankind to wake up to our plight and open our minds to a Universal consciousness that will enable humanity to resist and put away the insanity that exists here. They want humans to lay down the destructive patterns of abuse—systemic racism, global warming, social injustice, greed, war—that have brought us close to self-annihilation.

We are on the verge and are the closest we have ever been to joining the intergalactic community. As a species, we are at the beginning of a great evolution. Only through revolution can we lay aside the programming of the military-industrial complex and the forces that have enslaved us for many eons. If we don't commit to action, we will lose and be destined to start our evolution all over again. We have the technology now to change our path and have the capability to save ourselves and the planet. Earth Mother, which is a living entity, is going around in space and providing all that we need to exist. We must clear our minds and see the light. This is what I call, "The Revolution of Evolution" and we either evolve as a species or we die!

As I write this, the hands of the Doomsday Clock, which started in 1947, have moved another minute closer toward nuclear destruction. But there is no reason to be afraid because the Star Nation have vowed to help us. We must shake off the programming, turn off our televisions and internets, turn off our radios, release ourselves from subliminal messaging/programming, and get back to nature. Put the cell phones down, find space under a tree in the grass by a brook, and close the eyes while asking for guidance. Seek this knowledge find it to know the truth.

CHAPTER FOUR

Before There Was a Here

We are not alone and never have been.

All I can truly state is that I have attempted to use self-reference fleetingly because I am not what is important in regard to the message conveyed to me—through me. The message itself is what is important! Often, I have asked myself, "What am I doing here, or why am I doing this?" It feels insane, absurd, and trivial at times and I often feel torn to question my own sanity. But, when I finally lay down to rest, they come whispering in my ear. Waves of love and compassion sweep over and through me, assuring me I am on the right path, and I am doing what's right. They are here for me.

Again, I must accept the fact I have been chosen! There are many others besides me who carry this burden. Putting my fear aside, I take up the pen again knowing that I am not doing any of this for fame, fortune, or personal recognition. I am not important here as I gather my courage to continue on!

We are not alone and have never been alone. For anyone to believe we are the only life form existing in a galaxy of thousands of earth-like planets in our solar system would be rather insane. In fact, there is a fraction of the human race that is in contact with alien entities, and there is a certain faction of humanity that have been in contact with alien beings since the beginning of time.

With this knowledge, we have come to a threshold once again in our evolution as human beings. The only choice now is to join Universal humankind. This is a time to become enlightened so that we can turn the tide of corruption that has once again brought the earth and her inhabitants to the brink of extinction.

We must understand that this scenario has played out again and again throughout eons of our existence. The scientific community is only beginning to scratch the surface of this reality and has been kept in the dark just like all of humanity. This forbidden knowledge known only to a select few within a hierarchy, has been using this knowledge to gain control and power over the masses.

Humanity must acknowledge that the people in places of power have been in contact with alien forces from the beginning. But also, it's important to understand that many Indigenous and Native factions of the world have also been in contact with alien and spiritual beings from other dimensions, dimensional realms, and time.

So, now we have reached a point where we will discuss the inclusion of Lakota spiritual practices: *Wiwang Wac'ipi* (Sun Dance), *Inipi* (Sweat Lodge), *Hanblec'eya* (Vision Quest), and how these practices can help facilitate contact with otherworldly presences and spiritual entities.

Eternal spiritual presence, which is beyond age and time, has maintained contact with us Lakota people from the beginning. In a ceremony, I once asked the *Tunkas'ila Kola* (literally Grandfather friends, spoken together means Spirit Helpers), "How long have you been here?" The Grandfathers answer was, "We were here, before there was a here." No, we are not alone and will never be alone. Once we open the gate to the intergalactic community, we will realize the potential to save humanity and other creatures of the earth. We can now save our Earth

Mother and live in a utopia of harmonious balance with all the brothers and sisters of humanity as well as our newfound friends and relations of intergalactic communities. We are going to know peace on earth. It is important to understand that even though we may not be aware that these changes will eventually be forthcoming, the process has already been put into motion.

It is time to open our minds and our beings to the fact that we are at war and must lay down a course of action to protect humanity, the earth, and other beings inhabiting the earth. We must realize that attacks are coming from everywhere through the programming, subliminal messaging, and propaganda. Many people today are being imprisoned with this knowledge within their own being.

We are living in a time where the ruling society should decide whether humanity can handle the truth about what I share here, within in this book. I know and understand that the Star Nation mean us no harm and are not among us to take what we have, enslave us, or use us for a food source to feed some far-off intergalactic world.

The Star Nation is quite intelligent, friendly, and caring. This advanced state of being allows them to traverse different galaxies, dimensions, and realms throughout the Universe. I have pondered about these highly evolved beings and have come to one conclusion. The Star Nation is here to help humanity evolve because we have reached a critical point where we must make a choice. We will either join the intergalactic community or destroy humanity, all living creatures, and even the earth itself.

Assure yourself that if alien forces wanted what we have or wanted to overthrow the warring factions of the earth, they are quite capable of doing such a thing. Just recently on Facebook, I watched as some

Australian CIA faction launched a missile at an incoming UFO. I watched as the alien craft willingly scoot away from the missile, which began to fizzle and fall back to earth. This would now be considered an act of aggression against another worldly entity and no different than hostility directed towards our fellow beings. Upon seeing this, I realized that these are the very things we've been programmed to doubt. We've been taught to believe that they don't actually exist. Ask yourself, "With their advanced state of technology and capability, why didn't that UFO return fire?" In acknowledging this point, why is the earthling acting as the aggressor?

Funny as it seems, since having come in contact with my other worldly friends of the stars, I began to question the whats, the whys, and the hows. I will undoubtedly always be given or shown an answer, and when I feel I am alone in all of this, I am aware that the Star Nation is always with me.

As we delve deeper into Universal being, Universal consciousness connection, eternal being (eternal life), and fourth and fifth dimensional evolution, we will begin to understand the complexity of the truth of our being. We are at the point where we can choose to break free of the encumbrances of third dimensional being. It is possible to join the Universe in order to free ourselves and experience true universal being where the soul lives forever.

So, we know the Star People are among us and have been here for eons. They have studied humanity and even contacted a few of us, so it's only a matter of time before a day of complete disclosure is in sight. Having talked with people who must undoubtedly believe they will be traveling about in flying cars and spacecraft, the future seems bright indeed. What was considered sci-fi at the time will become our reality.

This is an acknowledgment that more members of humanity are being contacted and connected to the intergalactic community. We are the part of humanity that is "in the know" and striving ever forward to get our messages to the people of our earth.

As I sit here writing these passages, the Doomsday Clock has moved over one more second towards total annihilation and World War III could occur at any moment. Continents are already on fire, water is rising worldwide, and global warming is a contributing factor. Again, we are at war—have always been at war—and the last chance to save ourselves may be at hand. As I go about my business, I put my thoughts on this paper, sharing the process with friends, family, and groups of others who have been abducted by Star People or are in contact with them.

I was sharing my story with a friend, who isn't directly involved with pursuing the alien presence and contact. They asked, "If they are here, what could they even want from us (humankind)?" The answer is not what they would want from us, but what they want for us.

CHAPTER FIVE

Abduction, Vision, Prophecy, and Contact

When I found myself beginning to seek spirituality after a history of alcoholism and drug addiction, my Lakota people would eventually bring me to "the ways." In our language we call this the C'unku Luta, which translates in English as the Red Road. Learning these ways helped me to understand how to be respectful to life. Very early in my teens I was given a big bag of blessed peyote buttons, which seemed to awaken my being to the Spirit World. But in truth, none of these substances had any standing, as I witnessed many experiences later during my sobriety. The reality of my connection wasn't through any ingested substance. I learned that it was always present on the physical and telepathic level.

I received my instruction through telepathy and on some rare occasions, beings would show themselves to me. So, knowing and understanding what I am sharing here will always remain in this context because it's exactly as I remember it.

Abduction

What I am about to share is offered within a certain time and space. I am placing this event sometime mid-June 1985. An acquaintance and I, who I had met at a party in the small town where I lived, had gone on to his home a little further out by a nearby creek. Sitting apart, we were visiting into the night, drinking beer, smoking cigarettes, enjoying our newfound friendship, and we finally decided to rest at one point. Early the next morning after coffee and breakfast, my friend suggested we hitchhike to a nearby town, get something to drink and continue our visit; we had no idea what the day would bring or the event that would change both of our lives forever. We set out hitchhiking that morning and were given a ride from people who were going to the same place. After acquiring our packaged beer, we set off back towards my friend's home. The time frame at this point was morning, between 8:00 and 9:00. I remember it being a nice, sunny day in South Dakota.

Not getting a ride so easily on our return trip, we ended up walking the few miles down the road. We crossed over a bridge that traversed the river at one point, and we ended up walking over a secondary smaller bridge that was used for backwaters when the river rose. On this day, the river was low, and the bank was dry. As we crossed over the smaller bridge, we came to a point where we could scan the landscape around us. That was when we saw it.

Obscured at one point from the bridge by trees along the bank, we found it a hundred feet or so down the bank. Across the fence that ran the length of the highway, we both could see a rather large metallic object resting on the sandbanks of the river. At this point, the object was the only thing that held our interest. We both agreed we should go over for a closer look to investigate.

We proceeded to climb through the barbed wire and started to walk closer to what I would now describe as a classic example of a flying saucer as described in modern popular culture. What I was seeing was a somewhat metallic gray object that was smooth with no windows. It was about thirty feet in diameter and standing some eight feet high on a tripod of landing gear, as it must have flown and landed there. Mesmerized as we were by this, I walked up to the object and ran my hand across it. As I was feeling the surface of the craft, I said to myself, "Damn, it's real."

At that moment, my friend said "Look! Little people." What occurred after that moment was a mystery because I always draw a blank when I am traumatized. The following is what occurred for me, as my friend had an entirely different experience and memory on that day.

Once realizing there were other beings around us, I was concerned that we might be in danger. Just then, I was also realizing that I had walked upon one little person who had been bent down beside me. He stood up and was about four feet tall, with gray skin, big black eyes, nostrils not as a nose, and a slit mouth that was very thin and slight.

The being that I witnessed that day was the classic alien/Martian of popular culture and media.

There was a strange gap of time that I couldn't recall until early the next day when I heard birds chirping, which made me think it was about 4:00 AM the next morning. My friend and I were about 100 feet off the main road, which was quite a few miles from the location of my previous memories. We had been placed on a hill, with our heads upward and our feet down. As we both woke up at the same time, we sat up and looked around our location, taking an inventory. We looked at each other and I said, "WHAT THE HELL HAPPENED?" as I could not remember anything after looking into the alien being's eyes!

My friend started talking, "Don't you remember, they took us? They floated us into the ship, and we were taken to a larger ship." I tried to block out what I was hearing, but couldn't, since we had quite a walk ahead and he wanted to keep sharing about the experience.

Once we figured out our location and were moving in the direction of my friend's home, he resumed talking all the way back and said, "I called him Silver." I remember him saying we were examined and probed. I am guessing the man did not seem traumatized from the experience. I, on the other hand, went into denial, because I was convinced that only crazy people would admit to that experience. Once reaching my friend's house, I opted to continue to my own home, leaving him there to continue speaking to others of our experience. I left that day and never saw the man again as long as I have lived. To this day I am still missing eighteen hours of my life.

After I returned home, I examined myself, by feeling around my body, and the only thing amiss was a strange lump on my right

35

buttock. It has been there ever since, and I have never had it checked out, nor do I want to have it looked at. I never discussed it again until years later when I started finding other people who had found themselves in similar experiences.

I never realized that one day I would have contact and be connected to the Wic'ahpi Oyate. Hopefully, they will shed light on the plight of humanity! What is humanity going to do about it? The reality is that we don't have much time and we are historically at a critical point in our evolution. Either we get it right or fate will drive us back to the stone age or maybe even to total annihilation. We best get a grip!

I will do my best to elaborate my thoughts around this. The visions and prophecy will come up continually as my experience is shared and I will do my best to share the knowledge as it pertains to the significance of the message.

There are many things that have been shown to me. I understand that spiritual beliefs and the practice of ritual puts us in touch with interdimensional beings as well as the Star Nation. Thinking about these visions, though they are all intertwined and connected, I will choose the ones with the greatest message. I feel the most important encounters involved Beings of Light.

Vision

In my vision seeking, I usually fast from eating food and drinking water for four days. Hanblec'eya which means, "to cry for a dream" is important on the fourth day as one passes between different realms into the Spirit World! The time frame for this vision is somewhere in the 1990s. I was three days into my prayer and fast, and the weather had been nice. It was beautiful to say the least, though my time fasting was still not easy. I had seen harder quests and after three days Tunkas'ila would see fit to honor me with a dream and vision messages, taking me to a beautiful land, which was lush with a flowing stream. Tall, majestic trees, green grass, vegetation, and wildlife abounded and flourished there. Though I couldn't see the ones who had brought me there, I knew I was in their presence. They spoke to me, giving me knowledge and understanding as to why they had brought me to that place of wonder and beauty.

They spoke, "Look about you, what do you see? Look at the beauty of all life and your brothers and sisters of the *oma s'kan s'kan oyate* (wildlife) and all the living creatures of the earth. Look about you. They are all here, existing in a peaceful and harmonious balance as it was meant to be. They, and you, are all beings of light, you know?"

"So, now that you have a better understanding, we shall show you the light." And then, the lights came on. WOW! Everything lit up! Fluorescence was showing from it all, as the tree people were jutting shafts of light that had protruded from the earth. The light flowed up and out from their branches and leaves. The pines, maple, oak, and elm were glowing there! All the little creatures were glowing jewels as they moved about and the winged ones in the sky were like diamonds glowing in the sun. Even the waters of the streams were flowing, which were alight with life.

The creatures of the water and fishes were glowing like little gems and darting from place to place. All that I observed around me, the soil, the stone, and even myself, was all bright and flowing with light, love, and life! They spoke again, "See you now in all its magnificence the light and life given by *Wakan Tanka*, the Mystery. A breath of life for all, this is given to you to protect."

"Look over there!" As I gazed over, I could see a movement of darkness encroaching with a life of its own. They said to me "So, you see the darkness there. Acknowledge it and know there is a war being waged here, ongoing since the very beginning." As they showed me all the weapons of war, I noticed the objects of destruction appeared as darkness within the dark. There were black bombs, black cannons, and even the bullets were black.

They said, "See, these ones here were created in the dark of war; these were not created to feed the light but only to extinguish and put the lights out. You must learn to feed the light!"

So, the message was given to me. The two visions I shared here were a complete validation of the experiences that led up to my contact with the Star Nation and to the events that led up to that moment.

Although it might seem to the reader to be a bit off track, I included it because of its value to my whole experience.

Another vision quest I completed was sometime during the early 2000s, in the Black Hills in South Dakota. For more context, this vision is shared as a message from a Pine Tree, which we call *wazi* in Lakota. I had, at this point, placed myself under this tree and tied my offerings to the sacred beings in the branches. As I was fasting and praying, the following events occurred.

You must understand that I had concluded that all messages from the earth realm, other dimensions and time, and the Star Nation/Alien realm are Universal. They are one and the same.

In my fast and prayer, I moved from what we call the good red days and into the good blue days. This is what happens when we transition into the land of the spirit, which is about three days into the fast. My mind wandered at times as I sat there with my back against the tree and I thought to myself, "What a sad existence it must be to be a tree, never knowing anything of the world, knowing just those who stand with you."

At that moment, I was pulled from my body and what some people call the astral self was drawn into the wazi. That pine tree I had been sitting under was seemingly very excited that someone might ask such a thing or might even care. Finding myself here in spirit with my friend the tree, it spoke to me, "NO, NO! It's not that way at all. We, the trees, we travel also. Here, let me show you." I found myself being swept down through the root system and out into the earth, and I was traveling around and through an amazing connection of fingers along roots. I was seeing, what looked like sparks moving along the entire interconnected underground network. It felt like the way that electric impulses might move through the human brain. So, I found myself traveling along this trail of electron impulses through the earth and was amazed at the enormity of it all. That being was a worldwide connection to all living plant life on the planet and was a conduit for the Universal consciousness going on around us and through the earth since beginning of time.

I was amazed in my astral form as I was swept along with the spirit of the tree taking me to different points on the earth. Our mutual connection eventually brought us to a forest of bristle cones. Wazi said, "See, these are some of the eldest here." We then traveled on to the giant redwoods of the west coast and he told me, "These are some of our largest relatives." We also visited date palms in the Sahara, aspens in the mountains, different trees in South America, and other species all around the globe. I could feel the excitement emanating from my newfound friend as we were returning.

On our return, he happily said, "See! See! We travel too. We are everywhere! Not alone and stationary as first you believed. Only, I will say this. We are scared!"

I asked, "What is there to be scared of?" He replied, "It's the two legged, they've gone crazy. They are playing with fire and if they don't cease, we are all going to burn!!"

As I was returning into my being, I pondered these words. I had the feeling of the tree being me and acknowledged it as a breathing and living being of its own accord. Despite the feelings of the trees about humanity, I remembered having been able to converse at times with many of my fellows in the natural world. I have always been blessed with that ability!

Prophecy

So, at this point in my writing, it seems like a good time to express my understandings around prophecy.

Biblical, Buddhist, Native American, or other spiritual beliefs seem to have one thing in common: Humanity has survived flooding and a world of ice, and its final episode will be to face fire! As of 2020, there has been catastrophic wildland fires all over the world as witnessed in America, Brazil, Africa, and Australia. Many have claimed that this is prophesy playing out today in our times. To my understanding, this is truly a sad experience, but these manmade fires are the events that prophesy would foretell.

In response, I was given directions by the Wic'ahpi Oyate on how to build an earth-covered home and equip it with essential items. I would need to be able to house and feed my family because events unfolding in the 2020s would be coming from our Solar System. What we have seen thus far is nothing compared to what we may see in the future. These weren't just the predictions of an intergalactic traveler, but also ones who have time traveled.

The 2020s will be a decade of great change. No matter the outcome, we must pray that the prophecy and predictions will not come true and that we will never have to face a fire coming from the sky laying waste to all of established humanity!

Contact

After all this time and events that took place, I find it very hard to pinpoint exactly when I first established my contact with the Star Nation. It is even hard for me to determine when exactly I encountered the phenomena of an angel which I had a connection with, in my early years as a runaway child. I only remember having had the feeling of being watched and tracked by spiritual forces and other worldly beings. In 1995, I had a significant vision of tall buildings falling to the east. Visions since and before have made me believe everything is connected and that there is no coincidence in life.

In the next few chapters, I will share healing through the Star Nation, sightings, and encounters with alien presences. These beings were present during ceremony and I, as a common man, became a believer after having made contact with them. I knew that the Star people would be there to heal and help humankind with their presence. When asked to help with the sick and ailing, there is an understanding that they are here to help and aid us.

CHAPTER SIX

Forbidden Knowledge

In this chapter, we will address the topic of the conspiracy of the social elites and their leading hierarchy. Through the ages, they have notably not only possessed the knowledge of Alien Nations, but also of the technology and understanding of universal life forms co-existing with humanity in different realms and dimensions. This is not common knowledge. The underground governing faction has spent a great deal of time programming and controlling the masses with subliminal messaging that is bombarding and enslaving citizens of the planet every day through the creation of civilized existence. Standards of money, work, and consumerism are set by the hierarchy at the top level of their command structure. The rate that you are paying as you go about trying to exist is what leads you to live within an enslaved system.

There is a war being waged as we speak; the war's subject is humanity, the earth, and all creatures of the earth. Think about how 1-10 percent of the world's population controls almost 90 percent of the wealth and property around the globe. A hierarchy of such proportion, whose greed and corruption knows no bounds, puts forth a scenario of annihilation of the masses. The perfect scenario for this elite faction is a population of 500,000 people, most of them slaves, that will cater to the corrupt.

The Cabal is the 1 percent of the population that rules and controls all factors of life on earth using a "shadow government." The Cabal has enslaved humanity through the illusion of power and deception, using subliminal messaging, because they control all media. The programming has its effects, and the actions of elitists help to keep the hate alive. Religious persecution, used by the people in control, creates new enemies to feed the hatred of humanity and the war machine.

War is profitable, but at what cost to humanity and the earth? It's time for us to pull the veil aside and see the truth. There is a new generation who can see through the lies and deceptions. These youth will save the earth and the Star Nation will be here to assist them! God speed!

The year is 2020 and we are at war! Humanity is a step closer to total annihilation as we move the nuclear clock to two minutes before midnight. Massive fires and climate change throughout the world threaten many species that may someday become extinct.

There is pollution from plastic that is choking the oceans and marine life worldwide. The Fukushima tsunami crippled Japan and the nuclear facilities melted down as a result. Radiation was spilled into the ocean, which has caused mutations in marine life from radioactive poisoning. I could go on about the atrocities mentioned here, but we need to do whatever is necessary to save the planet and as we are closer to complete disclosure. We need to change our course and find a better way of being. The old ways of Big Oil and the industrial military complex have brought us to the brink of destruction, and we cannot do this any longer. We must return to sanity and save the planet and ourselves.

What will it take to make us finally realize that the only real friends we have exist in the Star Nation?

CHAPTER SEVEN

Walking Over the
Bodies of the Dead

My visions have been with me all my life. My earlier visionary experiences have to do with a tall shadow figure with glowing red eyes, but the vision I am about to share came to me in the mid-nineties. The vision seems significant today because of how the world is in fear of the Coronavirus.

In my vision, I was walking through a cave. The walls of the cave were pitch black and made of granite. Water was trickling down and in places, the floor was covered in green moss. I recognized the scenario of my vision, as I had been there many years before and had a very clear message in those early years of my development. As before, the way in front of me was clearly shown (like when I am wearing my head lamp to light my path). The only difference in this dreamscape was the clear path laid out for me, which glowed and beckoned me to follow. As I am shown this, I understand that I must follow it. Remembering past experiences in the cave, I was curious as to what awaited me this time. I didn't have long to wait as I gazed up and down the expanse of this large opening of black granite. I realized that the cave was filled with the scattered and horrifically mutilated bodies of the dead.

Some of these were headless, limbless, or only torsos. There was no respect to age, gender, or class, if you could include class in the mutilated remains of humanity. Babies, children, adults, and elderly were all lying before me with some in a bad state of decomposition. Others were freshly killed and torn open with their insides either missing or tossed about. I saw carnage and I questioned, "What is this?" I then realized the path of light took me directly over and through the bodies of the dead.

So, with the light beckoning onward, I stepped out into the cavern and proceeded to walk over the corpses. At some point, I seemed to feel them beneath my feet, which gave me a goose's sense of flesh. I wandered along this path to another part of the cavern, which led me out and away from that sea of carnage. (Note: as I recite my visionary experiences and/or dreams, I can only tell my readers exactly what I had seen at the time. What I saw had no prejudice to race, gender and/or creed, but was only what I'd seen).

I was led along into another part of the cavern, and I came to a place where there were columns made of the same black granite from the cave. The room was lit by torches, and I was aware of a figure in front of me. This figure stood in front of a black granite altar with columns jutting out of either side. I was aware that the figure had its back towards me. I was not sure of its gender. The figure was clad in long black robes with long blonde hair tied in a ponytail down its back, which was about two to three feet in length. As the figure turned to face me, I realized this was a man with a brown beard cut about six inches down and straight across. He had piercing, ice blue eyes. As I have never liked those eyes, I turned my gaze down and away.

As I looked in another direction there was something thrown at my feet that caught my attention. As I examined it, I realized it was a small bloody pelt of some creature and was startled to see the skull of some animal. It was a small, toothy skull, which had been freshly skinned there directly within my sight. "It's a cat," the man said to me, as he proceeded to eat the skull like someone would eat an apple. As he devoured the skull before my eyes, and I could hear the crunching of bone and flesh, I was left in wonderment as to what exactly that was all about.

The man in the black robes had turned his attention to me once again, reaching behind himself to pull forth a large leather-bound book. The book, almost two feet by two feet, seemed quite extensive with its contents. At that moment, what was in those pages was a mystery to me.

The mystery, however, was not for long, as I was soon beckoned to observe the contents of the large book. As I leafed through the pages, I looked at more carnage like what I had witnessed earlier in my visionary dream. I understood that these were glimpses of diseases. Then I became more aware that I was witnessing every disease known to man. These were diseases that had devastated entire populations, leaving survivors to deal with the burial and disposal of the dead bodies.

From the pages laid out in front of me, I was aware of the devastating effects of illnesses like plagues, smallpox, cholera, famine, and many that I didn't recognize; but these diseases were seemingly just as devastating as the rest. The book foretold of all the diseases unleashed upon humanity since the beginning of recorded history. The last page of the book was of a catastrophe, and the man in black robes voiced these three words, "This shall be." He then slammed the book closed in my face. I awoke startled, gasping for breath, and clutched my heart with this visionary experience and another message.

When I shared the vision with a friend later on, his response was, "Are you on drugs?"

I answered back, "No, clean and sober a decade now!"

CHAPTER EIGHT

Messages, Healing, and Contact

I am always in a state of wonder and pondering about when, where, and how I ever came to be in contact with the Wic'ahpi Oyate. In the beginning, how could I have known that I would someday become a friend and companion of these beings. They are always close now, watching over me, caring for me, and leading me on my path. They have been with me throughout my vision quests, Sun Dances, and all the ceremonies from the beginning of my journey and finding my way with the people. All of us that are on this Red Road are part of a larger rainbow tribe. We are all nationalities, all races, all genders, and all walks of life; we are seeking to find our places and niches in the Sacred Circle of Life.

I have a memory of the Wic'ahpi Oyate, from the early 2000s when I was Sun Dancing on one hot August day. It was the third day of a four-day pledge and many of us were dancing in a line and facing towards the sacred tree in the center of the arbor. One of my fellow dancers motioned for us to take notice by pointing upward. I gazed in that direction and saw a UFO that was suspended in the northeast region of the sky. My view of the ship was directly through the crotch of the sacred tree, and as we changed formation in our dance, I lost sight of our extraterrestrial observer. To this day, all those who witnessed that phenomenon talk about the year of the UFOs.

I have concluded the time frame for that Sun Dance was summer of August 2004. A day after the ceremony was finished, it was time for me to return home, and I had an occurrence that awakened me to the love and power of my friends, the Star Nation. I was at home the morning after the dance, which was always a treat after four days of fasting and praying in the arbor. I awoke to a bird chirping, the sun shining through the window, and a slight breeze coming into the house. It was a beautiful day.

What happened next has always been a curiosity for me, as I would have never expected such an occurrence to unfold in my being! As was my custom, I was sleeping in the nude and lying on my side. I had been pierced both in the front and back at the Sun Dance and had been lying on my side as I healed. I never enjoyed being stuck to the sheets from being pierced. My *hesani* (spouse) and I recuperated from the four-day ceremony and rested.

As I lay here on this morning, all of sudden, there was this tingling sensation, which began in my toes. Noticing this, I realized that this feeling was moving up and through me, leaving me paralyzed anywhere the vibration had touched. I lay there gazing at my hesani laying across from me, sleeping quietly. She was oblivious of the fact that there was something going on with me in that moment. While thinking I should awaken my hesani, I realized that the tingling had moved up my legs, thighs, torso, and through my arms. Upon reaching my neck and head, I was totally paralyzed.

Things that have occurred with me throughout my life have always led to questions like, "What is happening?" and then always, "Am I to be like this forever, how long will this last?".

While I was looking at my hesani lying there directly across from me, I tried to reach out to her using telepathy. "Damn you woman! Wake up! Can't you see there is something happening here?" As I lay there for what felt like hours, I started to notice that the tingling in my body was disappearing just as quickly as it had arrived. As the sensation was leaving down through my toes, I could feel and wiggle them once again. One more time the sensation moved through my body and exited through the top of my cranium, which seemed to have an audible, "Pop!" And it was done.

I woke my hesani who was lying there and told her the tale of what had just happened to me on that glorious morning of that special day. Whatever it was, I was still amongst the living!

At one point, I shared this occurrence with my brother, the Medicine Man, when I went to visit him. When asked what it could have meant, he answered, "Well it seems they healed you."

As I was leaving, I looked back and responded, "But, did I need healing?"

He answered, "Hmmm, you must have."

After this, I seemed to be in constant contact with these Star Nation beings or what we call the Wic'ahpi Oyate!

Soon after this, I started receiving messages and was given tasks from the Wic'ahpi Oyate. It was also during this time that my relations would come and go along the trail of broken relationships. I would live alone on this trail in the prairie for a great deal of time with my new friends! As they started having me do their bidding, I was always impressed that I could have a house full of guests with nobody awakening as I went out of my house. They would wake me up early in the morning, beckoning me to grab my dipper and pray with the sacred waters., This was six years before the 2016 Standing Rock pipeline protest in North Dakota that was defended by water protectors.

I was up praying to, who I came to believe was, the *Anpo Wic'ahpi* or the Morning Star. All throughout and up to this point, it would have me up between midnight and three AM. I had started to call this time the witching hours, as I would be singing and praying until daybreak. I remember one nice spring day in mid-March. I was woken and told to pray with the waters, so I filled my dipper, and stepped out into the yard to pray. On finishing my prayers, I only drank half a water dipper as I had needed to relieve myself very badly. I poured the water onto the ground and thought to myself, "Maybe I should not have done that." As I awoke to a spring storm the next day, three feet of snow had accumulated overnight, I remember thinking, "Damn, I hope I have not had something to do with this as the forest has been beautiful for days!"

As I progressed with my connection to who I have come to consider my friends, I awoke on a summer morning realizing that they were coming. My friends were there as soon as I realized this, so I jumped up from my bed and ran to the front door to wave at them. I realized then that I had forgotten my dipper of water and said, "Hey! Wait there and I will get the water." I ran back into the house to grab my dipper, taking maybe ten seconds, but as soon as I returned my friends were gone.

"Damn, they are gone," I said to myself.

In that same moment I heard them say, "No we are not, we are over here!"

I realized at that moment that I had always been accustomed to them coming and being in the Northeast. I was beckoned to the South and I thought to myself, "How did Anpo Wic'ahpi move in the sky?" The Morning Star didn't move; I realized the sky was overcast with the star under the clouds and hovering above me in the sky. I felt something behind me, so I looked over my shoulder to see another light. This light was the same as his, which was above to the North and as far away as I could see. I watched it pass directly by the one hovering and continue on its way south and out of my sight. As I finished my prayer, I said to myself, "This is not the Morning Star." This water prayer would eventually turn me to other tasks in my life that included my being involved with the Water Protectors at Standing Rock, North Dakota in 2016. Traveling about the country would become my new norm.

From time to time, when I would return home after having had enough of the road, I would still be visited by the others. It was on one of these occasions that I was visited by the one I call Light Being. I was home once again after a stint on the road, having come back from Standing Rock and other points on the map.

I built a fire and made a pot of coffee, and carefully eyed my food reserves. I made myself something to eat and prepared to climb into bed as this had been another long journey and day. What occurred at that point still makes me ponder as to what happened exactly that one night in the prairie.

As I lay there contemplating, I took notes of things that needed to be done and made plans for the coming day. As I did this, I realized there was something forming in the middle of the room in front of me. It was a figure that was almost human-like because of its head, torso, and limbs. From what I could tell it was not a human, but what I refer to as a Light Being. It appeared as light broken down into its spectrum when all of the different colors emerge. I noticed a light that moved in a zigzag pattern and down through the entity before me. As I looked at it then, it was a mystery and still remains to be so.

I asked, "Who are you? What do you want here and what are you?" I didn't receive an answer from the entity to my question. I asked again, "Who are you? What do you want from here? And what are you?" No answer came to me, which made me fearful because the other beings before this encounter had all answered me. I had a bright idea to close my eyes, in the hope that it might go away. However, I was proved wrong, as it had decided to enter my being. I could literally feel it inside of me.

In my next recollection, I woke up to a beautiful spring day wondering what had happened and if the light being was still a part of me at that moment. Either way, it never seemed to affect me adversely, so I just continued on.

The final phenomena I will share is something that occurred during my travels. Whenever I would reach home and was alone, things happened that would shed more light on my being. This particular experience of gifted knowledge lasted for four days. Once again having returned from a journey, I was told to remain where I had been lying down because they had something to give me. I mean, what was I going to do? They began to download information into my being, and my mind became filled with knowledge. I saw the past, present, and future as it pertains to today. That information included knowledge of its importance in my life. By the fourth morning, I was screaming for it to leave my head. I couldn't take anymore, and after I continued to scream, it finally ceased! I got up from this and was shaken, as I didn't know why I had been given that knowledge. But as the years have come and gone, I have always been aware that whatever is going on in the world around me, I seem to know it is going to happen.

CHAPTER NINE

A New Horizon

Brave World—Children of Light—Change Will Come

Now you may wonder, "What does this have to do with a message from the Star Nation?"

I would say, "It has everything to do with the coming younger generation. They will be the ones to usher in a new world and make the change needed to save both humanity and our Mother Earth in order to bring us into the intergalactic community!"

When I think of this chapter as describing the evolution of humanity, I would consider looking at science fiction from the 20th century. While humanity has made strides in scientific advancement, the corporate greed of the military industrial complex would like to squash any new progress. With earth hanging under the fear of a nuclear holocaust, the Cold War is still a real threat. What was once considered science fiction fifty years ago has now come to be true in our everyday reality. For instance, I remember a cartoon from that period, which featured the comic character Dick Tracy with a communicator watch that he used to fight crime in cartoon land. Back then it seemed to be just comic fantasy, but now I am living the reality of that imagination, as my granddaughter in 2020 sports a similar communicator watch/smart phone.

So, if you are grasping what I am getting at, then you understand one thing: What you see as science fiction at this time will undoubtedly be reality in the coming future. Wrap your mind around that. The only thing different is that we will have found universal peace by then. All the worlds-at-war-propaganda will be known to be an establishment lie and will have been put away once and for all. Eternity is the prayer

Don't for a moment underestimate the power of the coming generations. The Grandfathers have said, "The youth will make the changes." In my experience with the youth, they are evolving to create and are becoming more spiritually aware. They are not so much mutating but are instead evolving from a third dimensional being into a higher life form. The fourth and fifth dimensional beings are capable of all of this and are able to take form at will. I see this often, and I am often working with children who astrally project out of their bodies and have experienced meetings with spirits in the astral realm and/or spirit world.

We will witness some amazing things in the coming future if we can just save ourselves and the planet. My hope of hopes is that the old guard will die out quietly and completely from the earth. This would give children a chance to bring their ideals together to create a beautiful planet with humanity and all creatures living in harmonious balance with each other. This isn't just a fantasy. To understand this, it is important to look at why we are here at this point in time. Nuclear fission, petroleum, the military/industrial based society, and all greed and corruption have brought us to the brink of extinction! Our children, Mother Earth, and our Creator deserve much better. The naysayers may tell us that this is sheer folly, and in many ways, I hope and pray that they are correct. I wish that the idea that we, and all of humanity, could not possibly be at risk, were true. But in my heart, I believe that we will need a love greater than what humanity has ever conceived of, in order to turn the tide of negativity. Prayers are needed for the world and the seven coming generations.

CHAPTER TEN

At War with The World

This is a story that the Star Nation shared with me at one point about the ongoing history of the galaxy. It has been shared that great civilizations have come and gone throughout eons of galactic history. Humanity's journey on earth is just a fleeting moment in time.

Many years ago, I was told that Mars once was a living planet, and the Maya were a great empire based on Earth that had an extensive intergalactic trade network between here and other extraterrestrial civilizations.

The Maya had established a great, extensive, and powerful society both on Earth as well as Mars. They were intermingling with other galactic societies, with powerful and connected trade routes throughout the galaxy and between Earth and Mars.

The rich and powerful of the Maya society became corrupt, as what usually happens in humanity. The ruling class was at odds with the Martian hierarchy, which caused upheaval here and unrest on Mars. As it turns out, the Maya had nuclear capacity at that time on Earth as well as on Mars. Both planets were at risk of tyranny from the ruling hierarchy because of social turmoil and struggle on the Red Planet.

So, as the story goes, Mars was more like Earth than it is now. It had oceans, rivers, and greenery at one time. As a living and rolling metropolis, a planetary eruption was inevitable. The scientific community of the western hemisphere couldn't figure out what had become of certain peoples of North/South America who seemingly disappeared off the face of the earth. The Great Mayan Empire and the Martian Empire created travel and trade routes between both societies that were rather vast and extensive.

Like with any great empire, there was corruption and social unrest. The governing entity didn't find a way to cater to the citizens and there was a great upheaval on Mars. Warring factions on Mars took up arms against the corrupt government and their supporters. This was inevitable because "All power tends to corrupt; absolute power corrupts absolutely"[2] As the war on Mars waged on, it was apparent to the hierarchy on Earth that they would need to remedy the situation. It is said that the worlds were very war-like and possessed nuclear capabil-

---

2   Quote attributed to Lord Acton, a British historian.

ities. What resulted was a war between two worlds, and the governing body of Earth had a vested interest in Mars because much of its population was from our planet.

Now I would like to talk about the lost tribes of Earth that were unaccounted for and seemingly disappeared. I hope that the following story will shed light upon that. As the war intensified on Mars, Earth peoples started preparing for war. They prepared their ships for the journey and told the people of Earth to prepare for the battle as they would be traveling to assist their relatives on the Red Planet. The entire population was asked to join in the battle to hopefully overthrow the war lords and put an end to the conflict once and for all.

The warfare on Mars escalated out of control and the warring factions and the allied forces of Earth gathered to prepare for war on Mars. They had arrived to provide defense for their friends and relatives living there, as well as take claim of the planet and solar system. All the citizens of Earth collected together were summoned and put on ships to do battle thousands of miles from their earthly home.

As I decipher the things that I have been shown, I am aware that we are sometimes at the greatest point in galactic history to achieve greatness for mankind. However, we fall short in many great strides because humanity is willing to play out the same story again and again. We have fallen too many times just short of the mark when given chances for peace and love, which the gods truly want for us. Why we haven't achieved this peace is a mystery.

Why must we be at war? What is in humanity that brings out the animal in people? Though we are so intelligent and capable of great feats, are we still nothing more than a two-legged animal in space? I believe that this is an important question to ponder.

Returning to the story, the population of Earth had gone to Mars to fight the ongoing wars. They were fighting for whatever was the belief of any particular hour: "We need to liberate Mars!" "Free the Martians' relatives from the clutches of tyranny!" or "Save Mars!"

Did I mention that Mars had nuclear capacity? At some point, someone pushed the button and obliterated all warring factions, all relatives, and all life on the Red Planet. The Maya even obliterated themselves and left a wake of radioactive destruction that was bad enough that it would be a long time before the planet would support life again. Nuclear Holocaust is nothing new to the solar system.

CHAPTER ELEVEN

Praying with Humanity

For what it's worth, I am not sharing this information to lay blame or point out any particular faction of humanity, neither red, yellow, black or white. The sooner that we all decide to be in this together, our situation will improve. We are coming to a critical point in our development and must overcome the obstacles put here before us. If my message were to be misconstrued, I must apologize in advance, as I am only a messenger!

As I see it, life on Earth is under attack and humanity is at great risk now. We are now on the brink of extinction. I believe through diligence, protest, and prayer that we may be able to overcome the insanity that befalls us. My prayer for the oppressor, the war monger, or the one in power is to be able to see the beauty in humanity, all life, and our beautiful Mother Earth. I pray that the ultimate power reaches them and brings them to sanity. This is all I can hope for!

There is a movement coming to the planet as humanity is awakening, yet the threats of death and imprisonment only create fear. As we progress along these lines, standing up to the armies of the rich and powerful, it becomes more and more apparent that they are powerful entities. One thing is very clear. It's obvious they do not care for humanity, the earth, or any life forms thereof.

My life has been blessed because I was given the opportunity to experience the Standing Rock water protector pipeline protest of 2016-2017. I had the chance to watch as protestors ran supplies from California to the Standing Rock Sioux Reservation in North Dakota for the water protectors at Sacred Stone Camp near Cannonball, North Dakota. People from many walks of life under Lakota leadership were holding months long prayerful resistance against an army of pipeline oil guards. The sacred waters of the Missouri and Cannonball Rivers and the surrounding earth was at stake. When I first arrived after riding with my friends from California, after hearing about learning about the movement, I thought of the prayer made by the Wic'ahpi Oyate. I thought of how I had been guided to pray with the *Mni Wic'oni* (Water of Life) and the sacred waters for the last six years. After getting to Sacred

Stone Camp, I realized why I had come to this place at this time!

There was support from many indigenous tribes as well as foreign nations and delegations going to A New Earth Movement. There was support against the genocidal policies of rich, powerful, and corrupt governments, who used their mercenary armies against decent citizens of the United States.

We all witnessed law enforcement and private security for the Dakota Access Pipeline (DAPL) using water cannons, rubber bullets, bean bags, and tear gas against water protectors. Private security for the pipeline construction also used trained attack dogs against many indigenous and non-indigenous protesters. That experience was spectacular and beautiful at times, but it was also horrendous and terrifying as well!

I want to mention that the *Oc'eti S'akowin* or Seven Council fires, which includes the Lakota, Dakota, and Nakota Sioux, was in support of stopping the Dakota Access Pipeline from being built. People came from many tribes to make a stand against another breach of the territorial sovereignty of these nations. This happened above the land of the Hunkpapa band of Lakota Sioux and helped to create a grassroots movement that would soon gather support from around the world.

Their goal was to prevent a pipeline from being built that could contaminate the drinking water supplies for tribes and people along the Missouri River. The pipeline would begin near the Bakken Shale oil fields in northwest North Dakota. It would be laid across several states, traveling 1,172 miles through eastern South Dakota and finally ending in Patoka, Illinois. The Standing Rock Sioux Reservation was the land where a stand against the DAPL was made. The focus of our protest was Wic'oni Mni or Mni Wic'oni, which translates from Lakota as life-giving water or water of life. Many people from all parts of the world came to show support and make a stand against the construction of the pipeline, which was also referred to as the "Black Snake."

This proved to be a great event, as it showed the world that people of all races, creeds, social backgrounds, nationalities, and/or tribal affiliations could come together in a peaceful and respectful manner to protest for what they believed in. People participated in communal feedings, where all were welcome, and all were shown love and respect. It was an example of how humanity could actually live and exist in one place with harmonic balance.

At one point, the other side eventually showed their ugly heads. The oppressor once again demonstrated its might and hate by turning their dogs against human beings that were only asking for the right to clean water and the abuse of the earth to cease. Those aggressors who were mere employees of the oil empire brought my post-traumatic stress disorder (PTSD) to new levels of heightened awareness. The planes and helicopters circling around overhead let us know that we could be taken from the air as easily as from the land. We were all under attack and finally came to the realization that Standing Rock would never be the same after this was over.

It is said in the prophesy that came to the Hopi: "I believe there will come a day when people of all races, colors, and creeds will put aside their differences, they will come together in love, joining hands in unification, to heal the earth and all her children. They will move over the earth like a great whirling rainbow, bringing peace, understanding, and healing everywhere they go. Many creatures thought to be extinct or mythical will resurface at this time and the great trees that perished will return almost overnight. All living things will flourish, drawing sustenance from the breast of our Mother Earth." This is the Hopi/Cree prophesy. These days, I am eternally grateful and blessed, having looked back on the days I have experienced.

I was blessed by Wakan Tanka (The Great Mysterious One), for having been a participant at Standing Rock, South Dakota, during my time upon the earth and to have witnessed the coming of the rainbow tribe.

CHAPTER TWELVE

Winding Down

Since I was hoping to keep this writing within small passages, I wrote down, "short and sweet" on my original handwritten journal. I had chosen to complete this as a thirteen-chapter book and leave it at that. Things I chose to leave out were seemingly rather moot at this point, because my sharing of the messages given to me by the Wic'ahpi Oyate. It's really funny how this all came about. I now call them friends and they keep me as such, while listening to my prayers, and helping those in need when others ask for help. They have proven to be quite helpful and caring for the human faction and their care for me has been immense over the years.

As a loner, I had spent a great deal of time apart from humanity and by myself. Even when I am with people, in a way, I am apart. My friends, both extraterrestrial as well as earthly, have always been here with me. I have always taken humanity in small doses, because I haven't been the social animal that I feel I should be. Close friends, family, and extended family of mine prefer to be alone as well. When I am alone, I am more in tune with the Universe and closely connected to Nature and all of its beings.

As I often say, I am quite content to be on my own with my friends, for those who love and respect me will hold me dear in their hearts. They care for, and care about, me even though I am nothing more than a man of prayer and a messenger of gods. I am here on Earth with love for my fellow mankind and other fellow worldly creatures. All of life is dear to me and a sacred gift bestowed for all to behold.

Can you see the blessing all around you and the beauty of the life about you? Why would any seek to destroy or hurt the gifts bestowed to us here? Why would anyone ransack the earth and kill other beings to only increase their wealth, even though we have lost countless species because of the slaughter? Who are these people and who does this in the name of maximum profit?

A vision, that was recited some years back during a ceremony we had performed in the Mother Land, goes as follows: "There is a blue light that will shine over the land. Where it falls, humanity will drop to their knees and the spell will be broken. They will cry out as they know they have been deceived and the people of the earth will rise up. They will seek out the deceiver, the armies of the rich, who will also recognize the deception and lay down their weapons. Armies of the people will seek out the deceiver. The people of the earth will recognize that brothers, sisters, and all life are sacred. They will come together in a gathering of love and peace and find the deceivers wherever they have taken refuge. At that place, the children of the earth will build a great mountain of gold, silver, and money. They will put the deceiver in that place and say, "You! The deceiver has kept us blind all this time on your mountain of money. Now, you can join humanity when you have eaten all that is there! Humans that had once been blinded, deceived, and kept in bondage are the children who will finally heal the earth. The children of the earth will use technology to lift humanity and make a great society for all human beings. Humanity will find peace with all creatures great and small throughout the Universe."

The children of the earth will take back the earth and work to heal and replenish all that has been damaged to humanity, our fellow creatures of the earth, and the loving and caring Earth Mother! As I say, "Revolution or evolution, we either evolve as a species or we die." We have choices to make as we evolve.

Instead of largescale resources, my feelings lean towards acquiring our needs on a smaller and more personal scale. Since I have lived off the grid myself for some time, my feelings are personal. All of the great human thinkers of our time have made it possible to live in world without petroleum, uranium, coal, or other resources. These are the industries that are essentially poisoning humanity and the land. Power can now be gathered from wind generation and solar collection using all the technologies at our command. As we change direction with a brave new generation that waits for the old guard to die off, we might finally find our peace in the loving harmonious balance with rest of the cosmos. If we have the capacity to make the needed changes, the vision can become a reality, and we can save ourselves. We wait patiently on the cusp of a great era.

Economies that use industrial hemp, natural foods, sustainable seed, traditional wild foods, and free-range animals can help to provide a sustainable future for the world. There are also traditional forms of hunting game and offering prayers for harvest for the life that has been given so that we may sustain ourselves. This is living in gratitude for what the bounty offers and to be forever grateful in our hearts for the bountiful life we have been given. We can return to traditional practices, where all beings are cared for and loved: women, men, children, and elders. There will never be a homeless or unwanted person!

If my writing seems repetitive, there is a reason. Maybe, at some point, we will find the answer to all the societal woes we have created. This is the possibility of a dream becoming reality. As I now read the graffiti about me, I am somewhat given hope that there is a change coming soon.

Even with all the technology at our command, these passages could only be written by putting my pen to a piece of paper. As we evolve, we must understand an important truth. There is no death. There is only transformation as we finally lay down our earth robe (the physical body) that we have worn our whole life, while on this earth during this time. Since the soul is eternal and we pass from one place to another, traveling through and evolving, we are given a chance to join the fourth dimensional being. This state of being is becoming a spirit form and traveling throughout the Universe, unencumbered by the body. Or it is evolving to the fifth dimension to be able to travel throughout the Universe, time, and dimensions in spirit form. This is the place where you can materialize into your prime and greatest form of being. This is a future and an eternal life to look forward to.

Try to imagine, if you will, a world where there are rotary phones, phone booths, cassette recorders, vinyl recording, Pong, Atari, only black and white television, nine channels to choose from, disc, video players, MTV music… it seems like something prehistoric, right? This was the life and times of my generation. I mean really, we had it good, don't you know! Muscle cars, Woodstock, Jimi, Santana, the Summer of Love, and the beginning of the revolution. But there was also Kent State, Robert Kennedy, and other conflicts that included the end of the Vietnam War. But because of all the struggle and devastation since that period, it is time to put it all behind us and see our brothers and sisters as a revolutionary movement to help end all war.

We need to realize that our world, and all of humanity, is at risk. We need to clarify our existence once and for all or continue our downward spiral to the inevitable demise of mankind.

I quit dreaming a decade ago. Somehow, I close my eyes to rest, and I only draw a blank page in my mind. My eyes shut to the darkness and the day arrives like someone turned off the faucet to my dream world. It feels to me like dreams are the product of the common man and something I may not be able to experience again.

Maybe my mind works so constantly during my waking moments, that when it's time to rest, I shut down completely as though I have seen enough. Upon mentioning this to a friend, they said how it must be strange and hard to imagine not being able to dream and connect to that part of the psyche. I had told them that it was a phenomenon, and I wasn't exactly sure what it meant, but I assured my friend that when I do dream it has spiritual significance and meaning. I feel that it all has meaning to the writings here, and the images I am having to share with the world. What it means is never clear because I am not always given the answers or the meanings. The significance or the insignificance of what I am sharing here isn't necessarily known, as it could be a prediction or just a possibility!

In one of the dreams that I do remember, I was in the world in my dream, and I am sharing it as a part of the message bestowed with my writing.

In this dream, I find myself in some post-apocalyptic world. Somehow, I have survived the apocalypse and there is a small group of post-apocalyptic stragglers with me. We came together in the hopes of overcoming the destruction around us, hoping to survive and make some sense of our plight. Many of us ended up together as the last surviving society on earth. We were children trying to live in a war-torn world that was being stalked by marauding hordes of cannibals. We had to be wary and constantly move so as not to be discovered. There were many species of wild game and domestic live livestock that had also made it through the apocalypse, so those of us with hunting skills were able to make meat for our hungry and suffering brothers and sisters.

We were unknowing or uncaring of the radioactive content of the creatures we were feasting upon, and we foraged through the rubbish for clean water in the buildings that were left standing. Our group searched through structures where humanity had once congregated and shopped. As we dug through the piles of post-apocalyptic trash and what was left after the demise of our fellow humans, I happened upon a pile of fresh blankets still in their wrappings. I brought this to the attention of my friends, new and old. However, they said they want nothing to do with them since they could be diseased.

My thought pattern was that we all could have surely succumbed to the ravages of this said disease by now. Upon that, I helped myself to two of the blankets, cutting a hole in the center of one and making a makeshift poncho. I rolled up another for a bed roll and thus assuring myself some warmth in the future.

We continued on in our quest for survival, searching for food, water, and a home in this ravaged scenario. We had hoped there may be such a place for us in the torn, scarred remnants of human civilization. As we wandered aimlessly about the landscape looking for an undamaged part of the earth where we might set up some semblance of civilization, we hoped to once again hear the sound of children laughing and playing in the woods! We wandered a certain way for an endless amount of time and finally made a camp where we gathered at the end of each day to feed ourselves. The others built a fire for everyone to gather around to form a feeling of security and safety. I was leery of such extravagances and stepped away from the ones who had gathered. When I moved into the clearing away from the shedding light in our location and decided to lie down, I was suddenly aware that we had been found.

The cannibals were among us, and we were at the mercy of the brutal hungry hoard as they set about their carnivorous, murderous, and savage assault. We had been found and those cannibals decided to take my fellows as slaves. Some people were eaten immediately, and their flesh was charred on the dry fire where they had found comfort and warmth earlier.

I took up my bow and arrow and my blanket to flee into the darkness to escape the plight of my fellows. I ran for my life into the darkness to seek out a hiding spot away from the bloodshed and damage done to my people. I would never eat the flesh of another, so I knew that I wouldn't do well with the cannibals. I found a hole to crawl into, and all I could do was hope that I had saved myself. While lying there I listened to the screams of the others and prayed the cannibals would not sniff me out and capture me.

I awoke startled from this dream and was aware that the only dreams I have, may have some significance to my whole story. While I ponder this, I can't close my eyes for many hours. Not being able to close my eyes because of concern of what I might see is nothing new for me, and in many ways, not being able to dream may be my ultimate blessing.

I remember someone once said to me, "I wish I were like you, could be like you."

I heard that and my thoughts were, "No, you wouldn't want to be like me, nobody wants to see what I see."

I am dismayed by my dream and am left wondering what it may mean. The answers at times need more clarity. My heart asks, "Is this all for naught? Is the message given by the Alien Nation for no reason? Are my prayers and acts of love just hopeless and meaningless?

And then I find myself, all at once, so very weary and tired! What can all this mean? There is a mystery to it all.

CHAPTER THIRTEEN

The Message

This is the final chapter. Maybe we will then see what might come of it. I am just the messenger, and this is the knowledge I was given by my friends, the Alien Nation. If you were to tell my younger self that I would be here writing this passage, I would have told you that you were daft, for I never expected to live this long!

So, let's now return to chapter twelve, so you can understand my views on the significance of all that I have shared with you.

I was elaborating on the lifestyle of people in the 1900s with the invention of the automobile, the motorcycle, and other forms of transportation. Humanity was slowly beginning to evolve technologically, but the petrochemical-techno society would eventually make huge leaps that would take our world into a new future. Nothing would ever be the same!

The advancements would cast us into a futuristic expansion that was unimaginable 100 years ago. This enhancement would be a sort of coming of age for the human species! The computer age, smart phones, artificial intelligence, and satellite space stations were the first attempts to travel to our closest planetary relatives. Nobody was really aware that we had already had intergalactic technology for years.

With all the great advancements through technology, we are still led to believe the jet population is the only way to navigate the Universe, much less our own solar system. All the truly great inventions have been taken and hidden away from the sight of mankind. Those left in the dark are only given a taste of what exists, with just enough to keep everyone content and make it easier to program this society.

As I write, Coronavirus is wreaking havoc upon humanity and causing widespread fear and panic. It feels like we are under attack. We shall see how the latest phantasmagoric viral disease plays out. Everything we need to know of this latest plague upon humanity is right at our fingertips. Instead of moving forward as a people, the disease is keeping us paralyzed and in a state of fear. Few people are awake to the truth that healing people is not profitable for those in power, as we are fed propaganda. Though the supposed world economy is taking a big hit, big pharmaceutical companies and profit-making industries will surely win out in the end! Although this might seem long winded as it were, it is still leading up to some kind of grand finale.

It seems that we are easily manipulated, to say the least. "I saw it on Facebook, so it must be true, right?!" However, I am a believer in God, the gods, the Wic'ahpi Oyate, and the Alien Nation. My god, Wakan Tanka, makes this publication a reality since he has placed everything in order and given me the means to publish. You see, I am not a writer other than song lyrics and poetry. As a mechanic, I never would have published anything I had written, because it would be more prone to mechanical contrivance.

Again, I would only think to publish at the insistence of the Alien Nation and friends. As the messenger, it is with a belief that I share the knowledge of the written word with humanity and the known Universe! The one thing we need to understand is that the Alien Nation has been watching and following our species for eons, and they have never meant to harm humanity. They are willing to assist in our development to see humanity victorious in its next evolution, as they have witnessed our civilizations rise and fall throughout the eons. We, as a species, are on the verge of greatness.

However, governments' pieces of technology are meant to make people believe they care about the interests of humanity. In all reality, they could care less about disclosing any of the technologies unless there is some way that they could profit from them. They would rather keep the masses enslaved to the world conglomerate military-industrial complex. No matter how much power they may possess, people can't eat gold, silver, or money. The Universe is full of the metals, so intergalactic travel will be easily and eagerly acquired.

Do you get the gist of my message? With the help of four intergalactic friends, we will have the capacity to trade with new worlds, pioneer to establish colonies, and eradicate diseases once and for all. This is the future that our friends, the Star Nation, want humanity to experience. We could experience the gift of Universal consciousness as we learn to open our minds and hearts to creation and intergalactic truth and understanding.

When asked what the Alien Nation wants or needs from us, my answer is, "It is not what they want from us since we do not have much to offer them, but instead they want all of the creatures of the earth to put away war and hatred and to find peace and love in harmonious balance."

The propaganda you will see when the Alien Nation starts reaching out to us will be something like this, "The Aliens are invading Earth, coming down to take all we have and enslave humanity." Believe me, the Star Nation is by far more evolved than us and are not the body snatchers you are led to believe. They have had a hand in human evolution from the beginning. Some propaganda will say it is a great experiment, so we don't or won't eradicate ourselves once again.

There is hope and the Star Nation has given these messages to me with the commitment that we can overcome the wickedness that has held us captive for far too long. They have helped themselves to whatever they might need to sustain themselves all these eons and only taking what they need. They would never use the balance of nature because they recognize our planet Earth as a living thriving member of the Universe.

We must not fear the coming of the new age, but embrace it for all life, and take steps toward our place in a new awakening. We must take courage as we join the intergalactic society. We just need to overcome these lasts tests. The understanding is that we are awakening, and a great change is coming. It is among us here and now! We are on the threshold of forever and our new-found friends, the Star Nation, will be there for us!

AFTERWORD: THE SPIRITUAL MAGGOTS

The last tale that my uncle shared with me many years ago when I had begun my spiritual journey, gave me great insight at an early age. This teaching is one that I remember as a young man because it was something that I experienced and could relate to, as it explains the relations between all living beings on Earth.

Early on in my spiritual development, an uncle I was learning from looked at me to ask, "So, you want to know about the spiritual?"

I responded, "Well I suppose that's what I am doing here!"

He goes on to tell me, "Have you ever seen a dead dog?"

And I said, "Yes, of course, I'm from the Rez!"

He continues, "Okay, so have you ever seen a dead dog that is full off maggots?"

It takes me to a time when my younger uncle and I were down by the creek looking for medicine when we saw a dead dog in the water, full of maggots. I was amazed that the maggots could breathe under water as they devoured the flesh and got ready to pupate and become flies. This long-ago memory had come to me, and I assured my uncle that yes, I had witnessed a dead dog crawling with maggots.

My uncle says, "Good, good! So, you've seen the maggots swarming in and around the dead dog, going about their business and doing what maggots do. If you have ever looked closely or studied these maggots, you would find there would be hundreds of thousands of maggots. And there would be one that is doing something different, this is the spiritual maggot!"

This made me think about the complexity of all life and creatures and how each species has a spiritual seeker and guide. We, all creatures of the earth and cosmos, are more complex that we could ever know or believe!

GLOSSARY: PRONUNCIATION AND TRANSLATION FOR LAKOTA WORDS[3]

Anpo Wic'ahpi (ahn-po wee-chalk-pee):
   Morning Star

C'unku Luta (chun-koo loo-tah): Red Road

Hanblec'eya (hahn-bley-chey-ya):
   Vision quest, crying for a dream

Hesani (hay-sah-nee): half-side, spouse

Inipi (ee-nee-pee): Sweat Lodge

Kola (cho-la): friends

Mni Wic'oni (mini we-cho-nee):
   Water of Life

Oc'eti S'akowin (o-che-ti sha-ko-win):
   Seven Council fires

---

3   The Lakota language was originally not a
   written language. This glossary is provided
   by Gary Lee Christensen and may not match
   other printed or online resources.

Oma s'kan s'kan (o-ma shkahn shkahn):
  wildlife nation, that moving out there

Tunkas'ila (tunk-a-she-la): Grandfather

Wakan Tanka (wahk-kahn tonk-ah):
  Great mystery (God)

Wazi (wah-zee): pine tree

Wic'ahpi Oyate (wee-chalk-pee oi-yah-tay):
  Star Nation

Wiwang Wacipi (wee-wong wah-chee-pee):
  Sun Dance ceremony

Wopila (wo-pee-la): a giving of thanks

ACKNOWLEDGMENTS

I'd like to thank Teresa Marro for her help in putting this book together. I also want to express gratitude for my publisher, Michelle Vandepas. Without her, these works would not be possible. Finally, I would like to thank my friends the Star Nation who insisted we get this message to the world and its peoples.

Wopila to all of the people who have shown their support for me in my life. It has been an unending adventure of faith and humility.

For more great books, visit
Empower Press online at
books.gracepointpublishing.com

Made in the USA
Monee, IL
11 September 2022